Greeting Cards XL with Ribbon

Mieke van den Akker

FORTE PUBLISHERS

Contents

ISBN 90 5877 629 8

This is a publication from
Forte Publishers BV
P.O. Box 1394
3500 BJ Utrecht
The Netherlands

For more information about the
creative books available from Forte
Uitgevers:
www.forteuitgevers.nl

Final editing: Gina Kors-Lambers,
Steenwijk, the Netherlands
Photography and digital image
editing: Fotografie Gerhard Witteveen,
Apeldoorn, the Netherlands
Cover and inner design: BADE creatieve
communicatie, Baarn, the Netherlands
Translation: Michael Ford, TextCase,
Hilversum, the Netherlands

Preface

I was very excited the first time I saw the large cabinet cards,

because they open up a whole new range of options for making

cards. They are, of course, completely different, because you can

now divide the card up differently and use larger pictures.

In this book, I have used lots of different ribbons and many

different punches, as well as Marij Rahder, Megumi and Christina

cutting sheets. I have also used standard cards for those people

who still have to get used to the new size.

I wish you lots of fun with these new colourful cards.

Mieke

Techniques

Read these instructions carefully before starting to make the new cards.

Ribbon

If you want to add a ribbon to the card, then use double-sided adhesive tape to stick it to the inside of the card and the back of the card. Since that does not look too nice on the inside, stick a piece of paper of the same colour on top.

It is slightly easier to stick the ribbon on a piece of paper. You wrap the ribbon around the paper and stick it in place at the back. This can then be stuck on the card.
You can tie an attractive bow by making two loops with the ribbon and then tying them together. The ends will then point downwards. You can cut the ends of the ribbon off at an angle or into a dovetail.

Transparent stickers

Flowers are stuck behind the openings of a Quattro aperture card using transparent stickers. Stick the transparent stickers over the opening and stick the flowers behind them.

3D pictures

Stick foam tape on the card or the ribbon in order to make a 3D flower in a square. It will then look much nicer.

Materials

- Romak cards
- Romak paper
- Organza ribbon in various colours: 15 mm
- Printed Organza ribbon
- Pair of scissors
- Satin ribbon
- Stickers
- Foam tape

- Double-sided adhesive tape
- Silicon glue
- Ruler
- Pencil
- Marij Rahder cutting sheets
- Christina cutting sheets
- Megumi cutting sheets
- Cutting tool
- Various punches

- Sulky thread
- Adhesive tape
- Eyelets
- Adhesive stones
- Coloured split pins

The articles numbers are stated with each card.

Step-by-step

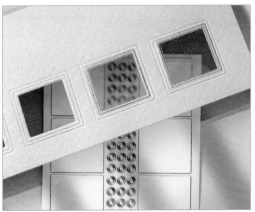

1. Quattro aperture card with transparent stickers.

2. Stick the flower behind the transparent sticker.

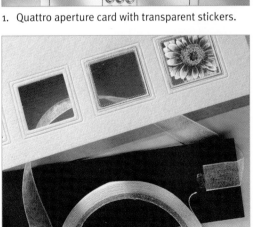

3. Use double-sided adhesive tape to stick the ribbon to the back of a sheet of paper.

4. Tie it into an attractive bow.

Megumi

Blue bow

What you need
- Portrait cabinet card: yellow (204-67)
- Megumi cutting sheet (P0-000-12)
- Sticker sheet: gold (1033)
- Paper: yellow 10 x 20.5 cm (901-67)
- Organza ribbon: light blue 15 mm (02-115-28)
- Satin ribbon: light blue 3 mm (02-250-28)

Instructions
1. Cut out the picture with the oval. Stick it on the card and make it 3D.

2. Stick ornament stickers in the corners of the card and use border stickers to join them together.

3. Tie the Organza ribbon into a bow and stick it below the picture. Stick two pieces of ribbon on the card with a narrow piece of ribbon on top.

4. Stick yellow paper inside the card.

Triptych

What you need

- Portrait cabinet card: lilac (204-69)
- Paper: yellow 20.5 x 10 cm (906-67) and olive green 3 sheets of 5.5 x 5.5 cm (906-60)
- Megumi cutting sheet (Po-000-14)
- Organza ribbon: pink (02-220-64)
- Sticker sheet: gold (1033)

Instructions

1. Evenly distribute three pieces of Organza ribbon across the yellow paper. Stick the yellow paper on the card.

2. Stick the pictures on the pieces of olive green paper and stick the ornament stickers next to them.

Butterflies

What you need
- Portrait cabinet card: denim blue (204-31)
- Paper: red 7 x 10.7 cm (906-23),
  white 6.4 x 10.3 cm (906-21) and
  denim blue 20.5 x 10 cm (901-31)
- Sticker sheets: gold (332, 886 and 3101)
- Organza ribbon: light blue 15 mm (02-115-28)
- Megumi cutting sheets (Po-00-11 and Po-00-14)

Instructions

1. Stick the pieces of paper together. Cut out the
   picture and use foam tape to stick it on the paper.
   Stick everything on the card.

2. Cut out a square with a butterfly, stick a
   transparent sticker on top and cut it out.
   Stick this on the card below the picture.
   Stick the ornament stickers above and
   below the butterfly.

3. Stick the ribbon around the card. Stick
   the letters on the ribbon.

4. Stick blue paper inside the card.

Zigzag card

What you need
- *Square zigzag card: dark blue (157-25)*
- *Paper: red 4.5 x 14 cm and 6.5 x 6.5 cm (906-23) and olive green 6.3 x 6.3 cm and 4.3 x 12.5 cm (906-60)*
- *Organza ribbon: green with butterflies (02-225-09) and olive green 15 mm (02-115-60)*
- *Sticker sheet: gold (1033)*
- *Megumi cutting sheet (P0-000-10)*

Instructions

1. Fold the card closed and fold the right-hand side back. Stick the square pieces of paper on the square of the card.

2. Cut out the picture. Stick it on the card and make it 3D.

3. Stick ornament stickers in the corners of the card and use border stickers to join them together.

4. Stick the printed Organza ribbon on the olive green paper. Stick the red paper and the olive green paper on the card. Tie the green Organza ribbon into a bow and stick it on the card.

Marij Rahder

Sliding card

Instructions

1. Use the incisions to slide the two pieces of the card together.

2. Cut out the pictures

3. Stick the pictures on the card and make them 3D.

3. Tie a bow and stick it on the card.

What you need
- *Sliding card: flower (209-6065)*
- *Marij Rahder cutting sheet (P3-102-75)*
- *Organza ribbon: dark green 15 mm (02-115-24)*

Cabinet card

Instructions

1. Stick the paper together and stick the ribbon on top. Stick this on the card.

2. Cut out the pictures. Stick them on the card and make them 3D.

3. Finally, stick the border on the card.

What you need

- Landscape cabinet card: terracotta (205-58)
- Marij Rahder cutting sheet (P3-102-73)
- Paper: ivory 20 x 3.5 cm (901-21) and olive green 20 x 4 cm (901-58)
- Organza ribbon: olive green 15 mm (02-115-60)

White card

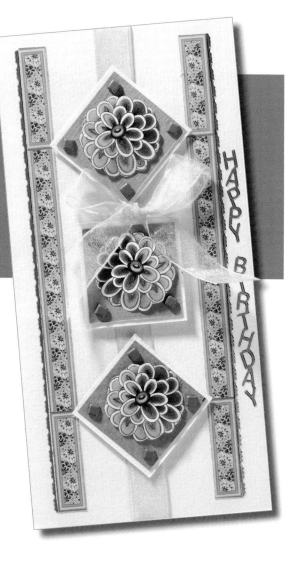

What you need
- Portrait cabinet card: mint green (204-65)
- Marij Rahder cutting sheet (P3-102-76)
- Sticker sheets: gold (332 and 1016)
- Paper: mint green 10 x 20.5 cm (901-65)
- Coloured split pins (10828/06)
- Organza ribbon: gold 15 mm (02-115-61)
- Paper: ivory 3 sheets of 4.3 x 4.3 cm (906-22) and olive green 3 sheets of 4 x 4 cm (906-60)

Instructions
1. Stick the ribbon on the card and stick the green paper inside the card.

2. Cut the borders out of the cutting sheet and stick them on the card. Cut out the flowers and stick them on the squares.

3. Make four holes in each square and place a split pin through each one. Use foam tape to stick the squares on the ribbon.

4. Tie a bow and stick it on the ribbon. Stick the text sticker on the card.

Trio aperture card

What you need
- *Portrait trio square aperture card:*
  olive green (169-58)
- *Marij Rahder cutting sheet (P3-102-73)*
  and background sheet (P0-102-80)
- *Paper: red 5 x 13.5 cm (901-23)*
- *Organza ribbon: dark green 15 mm (02-115-24)*
- *Satin ribbon: red 3 mm (02-250-23)*
- *Sticker sheet: gold (3186)*

Instructions

1. Cut out a piece of background paper (4.5 x 13 cm) and stick it on the red paper.

2. Stick the dark green ribbon and the red ribbon together. Stick this on the paper and then stick everything on the card.

3. Stick three transparent stickers on the openings in the card. Cut out small flowers and stick them behind the stickers.

4. Tie a bow and stick it on the ribbon.

Flowers

Roses

What you need
- *Landscape cabinet card: pink (205-64)*
- *Marij Rahder cutting sheet (P3-102-65)*
- *Organza ribbon: pink 15 mm (02-115-64)*
- *Punch: scales 40 mm*
- *Paper: red (906-23) and*
  pink 10 x 20.5 cm (901-64)
- *Sticker sheets: silver (1033) and gold (885)*

Instructions

1. Cut out the roses. Use the punch to punch four squares and stick the roses on the punched shapes.

2. Cut out a piece of background paper (8.5 x 20 cm) and stick it on the card. Stick the ribbon on the background paper.

3. Stick the text sticker on the ribbon and stick border stickers along the edges of the background paper.

4. Use foam tape to stick the four squares on the card. Stick pink paper inside the card.

Chinese flowers

What you need
- Portrait cabinet card: pink (204-64)
- Paper: terracotta 4.5 x 21 cm (901-58)
- Organza ribbon: pink 15 mm (02-115-64)
- Marij Rahder cutting sheet (P3-102-71)
- Sticker sheet: silver (1038 and 1016)

Instructions

1. Cut out a sticker (4 x 21 cm) and stick it on the terracotta strip of paper. Decorate the edges with border stickers.

2. Stick the ribbon on the strip and stick the strip on the card.

3. Cut out the pictures. Stick them on the card and make them 3D.

4. Stick the dragonfly in the middle.

Daffodils

Instructions

1. Stick the ribbon on the card. Cut out two borders and stick them on the card.

2. Cut out four daffodils and use transparent squares to stick them on the card.

3. Stick the white paper inside the card.

4. Stick the gold flower stickers on the ribbon. Tie a bow and stick it on the ribbon.

What you need

- Quattro aperture card: white (207-21)
- Organza ribbon: gold 15 mm (02-115-61)
- Marij Rahder cutting sheet (P3-102-64)
- Sticker sheet: gold (3101 and 886)
- Paper: white 10 x 20.5 cm (901-21)

Roses and butterflies

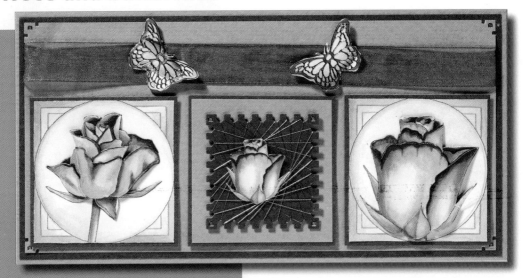

What you need
- *Landscape cabinet card: olive green (205-60)*
- *Paper: terracotta 10 x 20 cm 3 sheets of 6.3 x 6.3 cm (901-58) and olive green 9.5 x 19.5 cm and 5.9 x 5.9 cm (901-60)*
- *Snack punch (F2-635-03)*
- *Organza ribbon: olive green 15 mm (02-115-60)*
- *Marij Rahder cutting sheet (P3-102-66)*
- *Sticker sheet: gold (822)*
- *Punch: postage stamp 48 mm*
- *Sulky thread: gold (7004)*

Instructions
1. Use the snack punch to punch the corners of the olive green paper. Stick the ribbon on the paper, then on the terracotta paper and then on the card.

2. Punch out the square and wind the thread around it. Stick the roses on the terracotta squares and make them 3D. Use foam tape to stick the squares on the card.

3. Stick the other two squares on top of each other on the card. Use foam tape to stick the punched square in the middle. Cut out a small rose and stick this on top.

4. Stick two small butterflies anywhere on the cutting sheet. Cut them out and stick them on the ribbon.

Colourful flowers

Violet with a ribbon

What you need
- Square card: aubergine (099-26)
- Paper: pale blue 11.5 x 11.5 cm (908-28) and aubergine 8.5 x 5.5 cm and 6 x 6 cm (908-26)
- Marij Rahder cutting sheets (P3-102-61 and Po-102-62)
- Organza ribbon: dark blue 15 mm (02-115-25)

Instructions
1. Stick the ribbon on the pale blue paper and stick this on the card.

2. Tie a bow and stick it on the ribbon.

3. Cut out a piece of background paper (8 x 5 cm), stick it on the aubergine paper and then stick it on the card.

4. Cut out the violet. Stick it on the square piece of aubergine paper and make it 3D. Use foam tape to stick the square with the violet on the ribbon.

Violets

What you need
- Portrait cabinet card: pale blue (204-28)
- Marij Rahder cutting sheet (P3-102-61)
- Organza ribbon: blue with butterflies (02-225-28)
- Satin ribbon: light blue 3 mm (02-250-28)
- Paper: denim blue 3.8 x 21 cm, 6.5 x 6.5 cm and 2 sheets of 3.5 x 3.5 cm (901-31) and white 3.4 x 21 cm (901-21)
- Sticker sheet: gold (1033)
- Eyelets: pale blue (112405/0204)

Instructions
1. Stick the pieces of paper together. Stick the ribbon with butterflies on it and then stick this on the card.

2. Cut out the pictures. Stick them on the denim blue squares and make them 3D. Use foam tape to stick them on the card.

3. Punch two eyelets in the corners of the card and thread the satin ribbon through them.

4. Stick two ornament stickers in the corners of the card and use a border sticker to join them together.

Butterfly

What you need
- Portrait cabinet card: red (204-23)
- Paper: lilac 9.5 x 20.5 cm (901-69) and red (906-23)
- Marij Rahder cutting sheet (P3-102-74)
- Organza ribbon: gold 15 mm (02-115-61)
- Punch: scales 40 mm and 48 mm

Instructions

1. Stick the ribbons horizontally and vertically on the lilac paper. Stick the paper on the card.

2. Punch two red squares with the 48 mm punch and two lilac squares with the 40 mm punch. Stick the punched shapes together and use foam tape to stick them on the card.

3. Cut out two flowers and stick them on the squares.

4. Cut out the butterfly and stick it on the ribbon.

Green card

Instructions

1. Cut out a piece of background paper (4.5 x 13.5 cm) and stick it on the red paper. Stick the two ribbons on it and stick this on the card.

2. Tie a bow and stick it on the ribbon.

3. Cut out three flowers and stick them behind the transparent stickers.

4. Also stick transparent stickers on the back.

What you need

- Landscape trio square aperture card: green (192-24)
- Paper: red 5 x 14 cm (906-23)
- Marij Rahder cutting sheets: (P3-102-76 and P3-102-83)
- Organza ribbon: dark green 15 mm (02-115-24)
- Satin ribbon: red 3 mm (02-250-23)
- Sticker sheet: gold (3186)

Cabinet cards

Yellow card

What you need
- *Quattro aperture card: ivory (207-22)*
- *Christina cutting sheet (P0-200-03)*
- *Organza ribbon: pink 15 mm (02-115-64)*
- *Square punch: serrated 40 mm*
- *Paper: olive green (906-23), red (906-60) and ivory 10 x 20.5 cm (901-22)*
- *Sticker sheet: gold (1016 and 3186)*

Instructions
1. Stick the ribbon on the card.

2. Cut out four flowers and use transparent stickers to stick them on the card. Stick ivory paper inside the card.

3. Punch two shapes out of the red paper and one out of the olive green paper. Stick flowers on these squares and make them 3D. Use foam tape to stick the squares on the ribbon.

4. Stick a border sticker along the edge of the card.

Green card

What you need

- *Quattro aperture card:*
  olive green (907-60)
- *Megumi cutting sheets*
  (Po-000-10 and Po-000-14)
- *Paper: olive green 10 x 20.5 cm (901-60)*
- *Sticker sheet: gold (3101)*
- *Organza ribbon: gold 15 mm (02-115-61)*

Instructions

1. Stick the Organza ribbon on the card.

2. Cut out four flowers and use transparent stickers to stick them on the card. Stick olive green paper inside the card.

3. Tie a bow and stick it on the Organza ribbon.

4. Cut out a small picture. Stick it on the ribbon and make it 3D. Stick the wedding rings on the ribbon.

Pink flowers

What you need
- Quattro aperture card: yellow (907-67)
- Marij Rahder cutting sheet (P0-102-70)
- Sticker sheets: gold (3101 and 332)
- Organza ribbon: gold 15 mm (02-115-61)
- Paper: yellow 4.5 x 20.5 cm (901-67)

Instructions
1. Stick two ribbons on the card and stick the gold paper inside the card.

2. Cut out four flowers and use transparent stickers to stick them on the card.

3. Tie a bow and stick it on the ribbon. Cut out the flower. Stick it on the ribbon and make it 3D.

4. Add the text.

Violets

What you need
- *Quattro aperture card: lilac (907-69)*
- *Organza ribbon:*
  lilac with butterflies (02-225-69)
- *Marij Rahder cutting sheet (P0-102-62)*
- *Sticker sheet: gold (1033 and 3186)*
- *Paper: lilac 10 x 20.5 cm (901-69)*

Instructions
1. Stick the ribbon on the card.

2. Cut out four flowers and use transparent stickers to stick them on the card. Stick the paper inside the card.

3. Cut out the picture. Stick it on the ribbon and make it 3D.

4. Stick the ornament stickers on the card.

Spring flowers

Gerbera

What you need
- *Landscape card: terracotta (099-58)*
- *Paper: olive green 10 x 12.5 cm (906-60)*
- *Organza ribbon: green with butterflies (02-225-09)*
- *Marij Rahder cutting sheet (P3-102-69)*

Instructions
1. Stick the ribbon on both sides of the paper and stick this on the card.

2. Cut out the oval with the flower. Use foam tape to stick it on the card and make it 3D.

Cabinet card

Instructions

1. Stick the ribbon on the two strips of ivory paper and stick both pieces on the card.

2. Cut out the square with the picture and stick this on the ivory square.

3. Use foam tape to stick the ivory square on the card.

4. Stick ornament stickers in the corners of the card and use border stickers to join them together.

What you need

- Landscape cabinet card: terracotta (205-58)
- Paper: ivory 2 sheets of 10.5 x 3 cm and 7 x 7 cm (906-22)
- Sticker sheet: gold (1033)
- Organza ribbon: lilac Happy Birthday (02-220-69)

Yellow card

What you need

- *Square card: yellow (099-67)*
- *Paper: lilac 7 x 7 cm and 3.5 x 12.5 cm (906-69) and yellow (908-67)*
- *Organza ribbon: lilac with butterflies (02-225-69)*
- *Marij Rahder cutting sheet (P3-102-69)*
- *Sticker sheet: silver 1033*

Instructions

1. Stick the ribbon on the lilac strip and stick this on the card.

2. Cut out the square with the picture. Stick it on the lilac square and make it 3D.

3. Stick yellow paper inside the card.

4. Use foam tape to stick the picture on the card.

Amaryllises

Triptych

Instructions

1. Stick the two pieces of denim blue paper on the card and punch eyelets in the corners.

2. Cut out the pictures. Stick them on the card and make them 3D.

3. Punch two eyelets in the sides of the card. Thread the ribbon through the eyelets and tie it into a bow.

What you need
- Triptych cabinet card: pink (206-64)
- Marij Rahder cutting sheet (P3-102-67)
- Organza ribbon: pink 15 mm (02-115-64)
- Paper: denim blue 2 sheets of 8.5 x 8.5 cm (906-31)
- Eyelets: pink (112405/0208)

Blue card

What you need
- Landscape card: denim blue (174-31)
- Organza ribbon: gold 15 mm (02-115-61) and red 3 mm (02-103-23)
- Paper: denim blue (906-31) and red (906-23)
- Marij Rahder cutting sheet (P3-102-67)

Instructions

1. Stick the ribbons on the card. Stick blue paper inside the card.

2. Cut out the picture. Stick it on the red paper and make it 3D.

3. Cut it to the correct size and use foam tape to stick it on the card.

4. Stick corner pieces in the corners of the card.

Green card

Instructions

1. Stick the ribbons horizontally and vertically on the card. Stick a bow where the ribbons cross.

2. Stick blue paper inside the card.

3. Cut out the picture. Stick it on the red paper and make it 3D. Use foam tape to stick it on the card.

What you need
- *Square card: olive green (099-60)*
- *Organza ribbon:*
  dark blue 15 mm (02-115-24)
- *Paper: olive green (908-60) and*
  red 7.5 x 7.5 cm (906-23)
- *Marij Rahder cutting sheet (P3-102-67)*

Cards on page 1 and page 3

Sliding card (page 1)

What you need
- Sliding card: flower (209-2864)
- Marij Rahder cutting sheet (P3-102-74)
- Sticker sheet: gold (3101)
- Organza ribbon: light blue 15 mm (02-115-28)

Instructions
1. Use the incisions to slide the two pieces of the card together.

2. Cut out the pictures. Stick the square sticker on the card.

3. Stick the pictures on the card and make them 3D.

4. Tie a bow and stick it on the card.

Happy birthday (page 3)

What you need
- Landscape card: denim blue (096-31)
- Paper: red 9.2 x 9.2 cm (906-23) and lilac 9 x 9 cm and 9 x 4cm (906-69)
- Organza ribbon: lilac Happy Birthday (02-220-69)
- Satin ribbon with dots (02-250-69)
- Megumi cutting sheet (P0-000-10)

Instructions
1. Cut a 5 cm wide strip from the front of the card. Stick the red and lilac paper together. Stick the Organza ribbon on this and stick it on the card.

2. Stick the narrow piece of ribbon on lilac paper and stick it on the card.

3. Cut out the flowers. Stick them on the card and make them 3D.

4. Tie a bow in the ribbon with dots and stick it above the large flower.

The materials can be bought in craft shops. Retailers can order the materials from Romak in Hillegom, the Netherlands: fax +31 (0)252- 622761 or Kars en Co BV in Ochten, the Netherlands: tel 31 (0)344-642864. The materials are available from Van den Akker Creatief in Nieuw-Vennep, the Netherlands, tel +31 (0)252-687174, www.vandenakker.nl